Results Based Facilitation:
An Introduction

By Jolie Bain Pillsbury, Ph.D.

Copyright (c) 2013 by Sherbrooke Consulting Inc. All rights reserved. No part of this workbook may be reproduced or stored in a retrieval system or transmitted in any form or by any means electronic, photocopying, recording or otherwise without the prior written permission of Sherbrooke Consulting Inc. Results Based Facilitation is a trademark of Sherbrooke Consulting, Inc.

Preface

For the past twenty years people across the country have used Results Based Facilitation (RBF) to work together in service of improving the lives of children, families and communities. RBF is a specific, hands-on method that enables people to practice the skills for getting different and better results in their meetings and conversations. The method is useful in one-on-one conversations, small groups, and large groups whether you are a meeting participant or meeting facilitator.

The RBF method supports skill development by helping people learn the skills in a sequence where one skill builds upon another. The six RBF competencies in the developmental sequence are:

1. **Hold Roles** — become aware of how people hold roles in meetings and choose to develop the skill of holding the neutral role (when beneficial) as a participant or as an authorized facilitator.
2. **Hold Conversations** —become aware that conversations are the focus of collaborative work and to choose to participate in conversations with an appreciation of and openness to other people and their points of view.
3. **Hold Groups** — become aware that groups are composed of diverse individuals. As a result, they choose to understand each individual's perspectives, preferences, and interests, using methods to facilitate and support groups to have one conversation at a time.
4. **Hold 3R Meetings** — become aware of the structure and process of conversations and to choose to master and apply methods that will help you design and execute meetings that produce results.
5. **Hold Mental Models** — become aware of the range of mental models and choose to master and apply mental models that contribute to moving groups from talk to accountable, aligned action.
6. **Hold Action and Results** — become aware, that in meetings, groups can commit to aligned action and choose to work toward achieving meeting results that lead to organizational or neighborhood results, and ultimately, community results.

RBF skill development is also supported by providing methods for using the RBF skills as in the role of both a participant and a facilitator. Using the skills in the participant role is particularly helpful in building skills because often people spend more time as participants than as facilitators.

Participant Practice Guides are provided and give examples of how to deploy RBF skills when you are participating in meetings. The guides give examples that range from no risk to high risk. The no and low risk uses of the skill are appropriate when you are initially developing your comfort and confidence in using the skill. As you become more comfortable, confident, and experienced in deploying the RBF skills, the medium to high risk examples may be something you will be able to do.

Results Based Facilitation: An Introduction provides an overview of RBF theory and practice methods and a brief description of the four foundation competencies. For those interested in applying RBF skills at the mastery level, *Results Based Facilitation: Book One — Foundation Skills* and *Results Based Facilitation:Book*

Two — Advanced Skills provide in-depth practice methods and resources for skill development.

RBF reflects many years of partnership with colleagues who have greatly contributed to the the evolution of RBF skills. I would like to thank them for the generosity of their contributions and the warmth of their friendship.

- Victoria Goddard-Truitt for her contributions as a thought partner, editor of the *RBF Primer* and the *Theory of Aligned Contributions*, lead researcher developing the evidence base for practice, and codeveloper of the coaching and practice methods and developer of the High Action/High Alignment Assessment Tool.
- Raj Chawla for his dedication to the mastery and extension of the skills and as the co-author of many of the Results Based Leadership Applications and the author of *The Ten Conversations*.
- Steven Jones, Phyllis Rozansky, Ron Redmon, Kathleen Pogue White, and Mark Friedman whose work has contributed over the years to the development and application of RBF skills.
- Molly McGrath Tierney, Director Baltimore City Department of Social Services, Maryland and her staff or their application of RBF and leadership skills in improving the lives of children and families.
- Alice Shobe, Crystal Collier, and Olymphia Perkins for their leadership in applying RBF skills to improve the well-being of children, youth, and families.
- Connie Revell, Catherine Saucedo, Reason Reyes and all the staff of the Smoking Cessation Leadership Center for the successful implementation of Performance Partnerships across the country and use of RBF skills.
- Donna Stark, Barbara Squires, Jennifer Gross, and Ashley Stewart of the Annie E. Casey Foundation for the almost two decades of partnership and support of the development and practice of RBF. Many of the Advanced Skills were tested and refined in the crucible of their programs as leaders worked to contribute to improve the well-being of the most vulnerable families and children.

I also would like to acknowledge the leaders, too numerous to mention by name, who, by their willingness to practice RBF skills in service of improving results, have informed and made possible the development of the RBF skills and practice methods.

My deepest gratitude goes to Robert D. Pillsbury, my husband and cofounder of the Result Based Facilitation Network. This work would not have been possible without his helpful insights, unflagging support, extraordinary creativity as an iconographer, and lifelong commitment to being my closest thought and practice partner.

This book is dedicated to all the people who who get up every day and with dedication, patience, and perseverance do the hard work of making a measurable difference in the lives of children, families, and communities.

— Jolie Bain Pillsbury, Ph.D. (ENTJ)
co-founder of the Results Based Facilitation Network
co-founder of the Results Based Leadership Consortium
October 2013

Table of Contents

WHAT IS RESULTS BASED FACILITATION 1
- WHY ARE RBF SKILLS NEEDED? 1
- WHAT ARE THE BENEFITS OF USING RBF SKILLS? 2
- THE RBF COMPETENCIES AND SKILLS 2
- HOW DO I DEVELOP RBF SKILLS? 3
- ASSESSMENT OF RBF SKILLS 4

HOLD ROLES COMPETENCY 7
- THE PERSON-ROLE-SYSTEM FRAMEWORK 7
- THE BOUNDARIES OF AUTHORITY/ROLE AND TASK (B/ART) 7
- USE B/ART TO DEFINE AND DIFFERENTIATE ROLES 8
- USE B/ART TO UNDERSTAND GROUP DYNAMICS AND ACHIEVE MEETING RESULTS 9
    - HOLD NEUTRAL FACILITATOR ROLE 10
- GIVE THE WORK BACK TO THE GROUP 13

HOLD CONVERSATIONS COMPETENCY 15
- DEMONSTRATE APPRECIATIVE OPENNESS 15
- USE CONTEXT STATEMENT (CS), EFFECTIVE QUESTIONS (EQS), AND LISTEN FORS (LFS) 17

HOLD GROUPS COMPETENCY 19

Use Flip Chart To Display Group's Work.19
- SEQUENCE, SUMMARIZE, SYNTHESIZE 21
- SEQUENCE 21

Summarize.22

Synthesize.23

Check-In And Check-Out.24

HOLD 3R MEETINGS 27
- THE 3RS: RELATIONSHIPS, RESOURCES, AND RESULTS 27
- USE THE 3RS TO DESIGN THE MEETING 28
- USE THE 3RS IN THE MEETING TO ACHIEVE RESULTS 31

WHAT NEXT? TRY PBDM. 34
- WHERE TO GET MORE INFORMATION AND SUPPORT FOR RBF SKILLS DEVELOPMENT? 36

Important Icons

	Application of a skill		Mastery of a skill
	Awareness of a skill		Participant practice guide
	Checklist		Reflective practice
	Check-in or Check-out		Tips
	Exercise		

Glossary of Acronyms

3Rs	Results, Relationships, and Resources	MBTI®	Myers-Briggs Type Indicator®
ARE	Acknowledge, Rephrase, and Explore	PBDM	Proposal-Based Decision Making
B/ART	Boundary of Role, Authority and Task	PRS	Person-Role-System
CS	Context Statement	RBF	Results Based Facilitation
EQ	Effective Questions	RBL	Results Based Leadership
LF	Listen For	SBI	Situation Behavior Impact

What is Results Based Facilitation

RBF is an approach to designing, participating in, and facilitating meetings to get results. The RBF approach helps groups move from talk to action by focusing on meeting results and by developing an accountability framework for action commitments. The RBF process is designed to produce actions that lead to results within programs, organizations, and communities.

The conceptual model for RBF integrates approaches from Heifetz[1] (adaptive leadership), the White Institute (interaction of person, role, and system), Myers Briggs Type Indicator (use of type preferences to understand differential impact and to respond to group dynamics), Ury, Fisher and Patton [2] (interest based negotiation), Moore[3] (conflict resolution), and Senge[4] (systems thinking). At the core of RBF is the concept of results accountability. RBF is compatible with most results frameworks, and is particularly suitable for supporting the implementation of Friedman's Results Accountability Framework[5].

The following hypotheses integrate these approaches into a facilitative model of how groups move from talk to action that produces results:

Hypothesis 1: The work of meetings occurs through conversations and meetings are a series of conversations that can create meaning and movement to action and results.

Hypothesis 2: Group conversations can be designed, prepared for, and flexibly supported by someone with a set of listening and speaking skills.

Hypothesis 3: A facilitator working in support of the group while holding a neutral role can accelerate the work of the group.

RBF is a competency-based approach to participating in and facilitating meetings in order to get results. The six RBF competencies used by participants and facilitators move groups from talk to action that produces results within programs, organizations, and communities. This is done by focusing on meeting results and by developing an accountability framework for commitments to aligned action.

The central organizing concept of RBF is that of achieving results and accountability for results. Using RBF, meeting participants can:

> *Enter with results in mind and leave with action commitments in hand.*

Why Are RBF Skills Needed?

Results Based Facilitation skills are needed because many meetings tend to waste a lot of the time, energy, and talents of individuals who have good ideas and a desire to act on them. In your experience, how many times have you …

- ✓ Sat through a meeting feeling frustrated and bored?
- ✓ Gritted your teeth in a meeting to keep from screaming, because people have the

---

[1] Heifetz. *Leadership without Easy Answers*. Belknap Press. 1994.
[2] Fisher, Ury, and Patton. *Getting to Yes* (2nd Edition). Penguin Books. 1991.
[3] Moore. *The Mediations Process: Practical Strategies for Resolving Conflict*. Jossey-Bass. 1986.
[4] Senge. *The Fifth Discipline the Art and Practice of the Learning Organization*. Doubleday. 1990.
[5] Friedman. *Trying Hard Is Not Good Enough*. Trafford Publishing. 2005.

same conversation over and over?
- ✓ Done everything you could to avoid going to a meeting because you know your time would be better spent doing your own work in your own way?
- ✓ Checked out during a meeting and doodled, used your smartphone, read something, or daydreamed?

Through these experiences, you may have noticed that frustrating and boring meetings can actually make things worse. The premise of RBF books is that these experiences and feelings are the unintended consequences of meetings conducted in an unproductive way. Because of these negative, unintended consequences, unproductive meetings can be worse than no meeting at all. No one sets out to have a frustrating, boring, useless meeting, but this sad state of affairs is all too common.

One solution is to have no meetings or very few, thus limiting the pain of attending boring and frustrating meetings. However, this can limit the gains that are possible. Many urgent and important issues in our organizational and community lives can only be solved by people working together creatively and effectively.

What Are the Benefits of Using RBF Skills?

If you are experiencing these kinds of meetings, then you may need RBF skills (and an understanding of related theories), so you can have productive meetings that move people from talking to taking action that produces results. People who must work together to address urgent and important issues need a way to hold productive meetings that lead to positive outcomes, such as:

- ✓ stronger relationships
  - ✓ clearer communication
    - ✓ active participation
      - ✓ shared learning
        - ✓ exciting insights
          - ✓ creative problem solving
            - ✓ robust solution development
              - ✓ helpful conflict resolution
                - ✓ effective decision making
                  - ✓ commitment to action
                    - ✓ follow-through on commitments to action that produce results

RBF is one way to hold productive meetings. As a meeting participant, convener, or facilitator, you can integrate and apply RBF approaches and skills to your work.

THE RBF COMPETENCIES AND SKILLS

RBF consists of six competencies that enable groups to act collaboratively, make decisions together, identify how they can contribute to achieve observable results, and commit to take actions in an aligned way outside of the meeting. The six RBF competencies are the ability to: (1) Hold roles; (2) Hold conversations; (3) Hold groups; (4) Hold 3R meetings; (5) Hold mental models; and (6) Hold action and results. The first four competencies are the subject of *Book One — Foundation Skills*;

the last two, the subject of *Book Two — Advanced Skills*. The six competencies and the associated 22 distinct skills are listed in Table 1.

Table 1: The 6 RBF Competencies and 22 Skills

RBF Competencies and Skills
Hold Roles: *be aware of and make choices about roles that contribute to meeting results*
Use B/ART to define and differentiate roles
Use B/ART to understand group dynamics and achieve meeting results
Hold neutral facilitator role
Give the work back to the group
Hold Conversations: *listen with curiosity and attentiveness to frame dialogues that move to achieving results*
Demonstrate appreciative openness
Use Context Statements, Effective Questions, Listen Fors
Hold Groups: *support groups in having focused conversations that move to achieving results*
Use flip chart to display group's work
Sequence
Summarize
Synthesize
Check-in and Check-out
Hold 3R Meetings: *use the 3Rs to design and facilitate meetings that move groups from talk to action*
Use the 3Rs to design the meeting
Use the 3Rs in the meeting to achieve results
Hold Mental Models: *use a repertoire of perspectives that contribute to results*
Use PBDM to move groups from talk to action
Use conversations to develop convergence
Name and address barriers to convergence
Make and help others make action commitments
Be and help others be accountable for action commitments
Observe and respond to group dynamics
Assess and address conflict
Hold Action and Results: *make a difference in programs and community populations*
Be accountable in role for contributions to results
Use RBF skills to work collaboratively to accelerate progress toward results

How do I develop RBF skills?

Your development begins with a self-assessment of where you are now in your awareness and practice of the RBF skills. Based on this assessment, you will have the opportunity to learn, practice, and enhance your skills through reflection, application, and the use of feedback. The stages of development include gaining an awareness of the skills and the underlying theory, practicing the skills, and making the skills your own.

Mastery of the skills demands patience and discipline to understand the theory and integrate the skills. However, by understanding the theory and practicing the skills you will be able to contribute to people working well together, and begin to see how productive meetings can contribute to achieving good things in the organizations and communities you care about.

ASSESSMENT OF RBF SKILLS

Each of the 22 skills are described in terms of three levels of mastery:

- ✓ Developing Awareness — a beginning understanding of the concepts from reading or observation and a rudimentary command of the skills;
- ✓ Sill Application — a deeper and broader understanding of the skills and the ability to use the skills well in many situations; and,
- ✓ Sustaining Mastery — a comprehensive understanding of the skills and the ability to consistently integrate the skills in daily work and most situations.

In this introduction to RBF, each skill will list a brief description of each of the three levels and some effective questions that may help you assess where you are along the continuum. Although the application and mastery are presented, the focus of this book is on awareness.

Use Appendix C to assess where you are in the RBF developmental continuum. It is not expected that you will know all of the terms or skills during this preliminary assessment. If you are not yet familiar with the skill or the terms, you are beginning to develop awareness through the use of the assessment.

- Use the skills
- Get feedback (SBI) and coaching

- Apply the theory
- Identify how to improve skills based on the theory

- Observe the skill
- Practice the kill
- Seeing meeting results

- Self-assess
- Observe impact of use of the skill
- Identify skills for development

The Experiential Learning Cycle

Feedback and Coaching Support Skill Development

The primary practice method for skill development in the experiential learning cycle is to receive feedback and coaching. RBF makes a distinction between feedback and coaching and provides a specific method of giving and receiving feedback to accelerate skill development. The specific feedback method is called *situation, behavior, impact* or SBI[6].

---

[6] A description of the more general use of SBI, as originally developed by the Center for Creative Leadership, can be found at www.ccl.org/leadership/pdf/community/SBIJOBAID.pdf.

RBF Feedback

Feedback is information about behavior that is given in the present so that it may influence the way people behave in the future. It involves giving information that can be helpful to the people receiving the feedback. It helps them make choices about their own performance without telling them what to do. Advice is not feedback.

Advice is an opinion that is offered as something that is worthy to be followed, i.e., counsel. Usually advice is about "shoulds." Advice is often unsolicited, unappreciated, and ignored.

Feedback is about observation. It is timely and specific. Feedback includes the impact created, e.g., reactions and perceptions. It describes but does not judge. Feedback is different from criticism or praise — it is not evaluative.

feedback: When you started the meeting, the question on the chart was clearly written, but when you read the question your voice was low and I couldn't hear you.

criticism: You communicated poorly.

praise: You communicated well.

Differential Impact

Receiving feedback is best done by focusing on hearing it clearly, expressing appreciation for the information, then giving yourself time to process what you have heard before you choose what to do with the information. In receiving feedback, do not to try explain what you were trying to do or why — accept the feedback as it is offered.

Keep in mind that two people experiencing the same behavior from you may react differently. With this awareness of differential impact, you can choose how to use or not use the feedback to inform your practice and development.

SBI: A Model of Constructive Feedback

To develop RBF skills you will use a specific method of feedback — *Situation, Behavior, Impact* (SBI) — to provide feedback to others and to request feedback from others. SBI provides information about the impact of the behaviors associated with the use of RBF skills. SBI focuses the practice on skill improvement and illuminates differential impact.

S   Describe the Situation – Specify the situation in which the behavior occurred. Describe when and where the behavior occurred. The more specific details you can use in bringing the situation to mind, the clearer your feedback will be.

Do say: When you turned away to flip chart as we were discussing norms ...

Don't say: When you were facilitating ...

B   Describe the Behavior (Not an Interpretation of That Behavior) –
Behavior is a person's action; behavior is described using verbs (action words).

Do say: You lost eye contact with the group for several minutes.

Don't say: Turning your back was poor practice.

I   Describe the Impact the Other Person's Behavior Had on You – Impact statements offer candid (authentic, accurate) feedback of your emotional response and how that emotion affected your participation in the conversation.

> Do say: *When you turned away to flip chart you lost eye contact with the group. During that time, everyone was speaking at once, and I couldn't figure out how to get my voice heard. It made me feel unappreciated and I withdrew from the conversation.*
>
> Don't say: *The conversation fell apart.*

The practice method that accelerates the development of RBF skills includes: (1) skill practice followed by appreciative self-assessment; (2) feedback using SBI shared by those who experienced the skill practice; and (3) listening deeply to the SBI feedback and not question or contest the feedback, rather use it to develop greater awareness of differential impact. SBI practice method can illuminate differential impact of the same behavior on two different participants. For example:

S: When you were checking to see who wanted to speak at the beginning of the meeting

B: You said to a participant, *You haven't raised your hand, however, I may be reading something from your expression — do you want to speak?*

I: They responded, *I appreciated being asked, I realized I did have something to say and was comfortable saying it.*

I: From another participant: *I got concerned when you asked Ann if she wanted to speak, I wasn't ready to share and was anxious you would also ask me.*

The following form can be used to provide SBI feedback in RBF workshops. It is also appropriate for use in coaching and peer feedback environments.

Facilitator observed: _____	**Date/Time:** _____
Your name: _____	**MBTI type:** _____
Your Role during the Facilitation*: _____	

Situation (when and where):

Behavior (specific description of what you observed the facilitator say or do):

Impact (the impact on you in role: what you felt or thought in response to the situation and behavior of the facilitator and how it affected your participation):

* The role you have in a group or in relation to the other group members and/or the facilitator informs how you experience another person's behavior. For example, when in a supervisor role, you may be more sensitive to behavior that might challenge your authority than when you are in a peer role.

RBF Coaching

RBF coaching is specific to the RBF skills and is only done with permission from the person receiving the coaching. Coaching supplements self-assessment and SBI to accelerate skill building. Coaching is best done by those who have reached mastery in the RBF skills and have experience using the RBF coaching approach and practice methods.

Introduction to RBF

HOLD ROLES COMPETENCY

Be aware of and make choices about roles that contribute to achieving results

The Hold Roles competency includes the four skills:

1. Use B/ART to define and differentiate roles as they relate to meeting results.
2. Use B/ART to understand group dynamics and achieve meeting results.
3. Hold neutral facilitator role.
4. Give the work back to the group.

THE PERSON-ROLE-SYSTEM FRAMEWORK

For the RBF skills to be worth learning, it is necessary to see how, when, and to what end those skills can be used effectively in different roles. An understanding of how a person in a particular role might be authorized to accomplish a task using an RBF skill is a first step toward mastery of the Hold Roles competency. The awareness of the person in a role and his or her role in a system is the underlying concept of the person-role-system framework. Figure 1 shows the person-centric view of this concept.

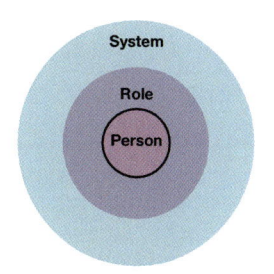

Fig. 1: Person-Role-System Framework

The Person-Role-System framework posits that a person's choices and actions are influenced by who they are as a unique individual and by roles they play (consciously and unconsciously) in different systems. This concept is illustrated in Figure 2. For example, one person might simultaneously be a father or mother in their family system, a member of the neighborhood watch in his or her local community system, a supervisor of a unit in his or her organizational system, and member of a cross-sector collaborative in a community-wide system.

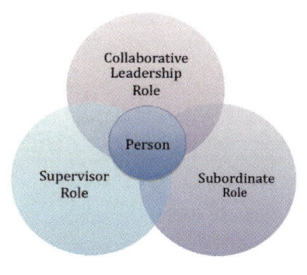

Fig. 2: A Person in Multiple Roles

THE BOUNDARIES OF AUTHORITY/ROLE and TASK (B/ART)

With the awareness the Person-Role-System comes the ability to see that in different roles people have different tasks with different authorities to do those tasks. Figure 2 illustrates how the intersection of the overlapping boundaries define a person's authority, role, and task in any particular situation.[7]

For example, a father or mother's task and authority relate to raising children. A neighborhood watch member's task and authority relate to ensuring the safety of the neighborhood. A supervisor's task and authority relate to managing the performance of a unit.

Notice that in each instance the task — parenting, safety patrol, management and oversight — *defines* the necessary authority to operate in that role and also *sets the limits* of that authority. For example, parents are authorized to parent only their own children (unless they have explicit permission to parent other children). A

---

[7] Green and Molenkamp. *The BART System of Group and Organizational Analysis*. 2005.

neighborhood watch member is authorized to patrol only his or her neighborhood. A supervisor is authorized to manage only the people in his or her unit.

These limits create boundaries for authority, role, and task. Similarly, meeting participants have roles (formal and informal, conscious and unconscious) that they play. These roles vary by the type of meeting and who the other participants are. Your awareness of your multiple roles enables you to apply the person-role-system framework and use the concepts of B/ART to guide where, when, and how to use RBF skills to contribute to meeting results.

Use B/ART to Define and Differentiate Roles

Awareness	Application	Mastery
Understands the concept of B/ART	Consciously establishes role in groups	Uses awareness of B/ART to contribute to meeting results and move from talk to action
• Do I understand the Person-Role-System framework? • Do I know and can I name my own B/ART in my daily work and in meetings?	• Do I comfortably name my role in meetings? • Do I understand the differences in my various roles?	• Do I consciously make choices to hold my stated role during a meeting? • Do I use my understanding of B/ART to align my actions with others to achieve results?

Every individual plays a number of roles in meetings and in organizations. Figure 2 illustrates the overlapping nature of the roles. For example, a person may have a consulting role in an organization and in that role have the authority to offer advice and information in their area of expertise. However, if the work of a particular meeting is not in that individual's area of expertise, he or she would be present in the role of a participant and not hold consultant authority. Your role defines your task and your authority to accomplish your task. Understanding the boundaries of task and authority for different roles enables you to hold your role in meetings. Analyzing different roles helps you deepen your understanding of how to apply the concept of B/ART and to work consciously within the B/ART of each role. Most people shift roles many times a day and *unconsciously* reorient their behavior and interactions to each situation. This RBF skill helps make the process *conscious* and to provide labels for the distinctions in B/ART.

B/ART: Lens for Understanding Group Dynamics

B/ART provides a lens for understanding group dynamics and the relationships of group members to each other. Each person is unique, having his or her preferences, gifts, and talents. However, each person's behaviors in a group are influenced by the roles he or she plays within formal and informal systems and his or her preferences and experiences.

A person might express him- or herself differently depending on the role held a particular moment. The same person might have a different demeanor as a supervisor with subordinates than when with their peers from another organization. Further, the customary expected, behavior of a supervisor might look and feel different in different systems. Take a minute and reflect on the questions below about Person-Role-System to illuminate the interaction of these factors in how you and others hold roles in meetings.

Reflective Practice: Person-Role-System

Person
- How might the factors of age, gender, race, ethnicity, cultural identity, MBTI preference, family and community background, or education and professional experience influence your exercise of authority in meetings?

Role
- When you are a participant in a meeting, what influences your comfort with and confidence in exercising your formal and/or informal authority?
- How often, if ever, are you a meeting facilitator?

System
- What are some of the systems in which you play a role (family, community, organizational)?
- How do those systems influence the role or roles you play in meetings (family meetings, community meetings, organizational meetings)?

Role in System
- What are the opportunities and challenges for you to use RBF skills in your roles in your systems?

Participant Practice Guide — Using B/ART to Define and Differentiate Roles

No Risk	Low Risk	Medium Risk	High Risk
Do a B/ART analysis for yourself and others prior to a meeting as part of your own preparation.	Hold your own B/ART consciously. When listening or speaking to others, consciously attend to their B/ART.	Name your own B/ART out loud as a context for making a proposal to the group.	Name out loud an inconsistency between a person's assumed authority in a meeting and his or her B/ART, as determined by the organization or the group.

Use B/ART to Understand Group Dynamics and Achieve Meeting Results

Awareness	Application	Mastery
Applies the concept of B/ART to understand group dynamics	Applies B/ART insights to assist groups in identifying and achieving meeting results	Accurately identifies B/ART issues and brings these issues to the group's awareness
• Do I use the person-role-system framework to assess the B/ART of meeting participants and consider how their B/ART will affect their participation?	• Do I clarify or help the group clarify the alignment of meeting results with the B/ART of the participants? • Do I model awareness of B/ART in meetings?	• Do I see how B/ART is affecting the groups' work and then use labeling, inquiry or hypotheses to illuminate the issues for the group? • Do I map who in the group holds the B/ART to address issues, make decisions and move to action?

In preparing for meetings, information can be used to understand potential group dynamics from a person-in-role perspective. Many factors such as age, gender, professional expertise or experience influence how a person will hold a role. The first step in applying the concept of B/ART to group dynamics is to be able to generate person-in-role hypotheses. The second step is to be able to build on that understanding and generate hypotheses about how role-in-system affects participation in meetings.

B/ART: Role-in-System Hypotheses

Using B/ART to better understand how systems influence people's behavior in role is helpful. Role-in-system is the perspective that enables you to see how systems that authorize or define a role, shapes people's behavior in role. For example, a supervisory role in a human services system can have a different type and level of

There is no hope of creating a better world without a deeper scientific insight into the function of leadership and culture, and of other essentials of group life.

— Kurt Lewin

authority than a supervisory role in the manufacturing sector. The supervisor of caseworkers in a clinical setting may supervise five to seven people and provide in depth supervision to ensure the appropriate decisions are made in difficult cases. The supervisor of workers in a manufacturing plan might supervise many more workers doing routine tasks and not provide individual supervision of those routine tasks. In each instance, the supervisor has the B/ART to oversee the quality of performance, however, the role-in-system perspective illuminates how the roles differ in execution.

Information can be gathered about role-in-system from many different sources. Organizational charts can show how the systems define authority and accountability. Titles can signal both function and level of authority.

Participant Practice Guide — Using B/ART to Understand Group Dynamics and Achieve Meeting Results

No Risk	Low Risk	Medium Risk	High Risk
Reflect on your B/ART relative to others in the meeting and develop hypotheses about how your B/ART and your exercise of authority influences the work of the group.	Based on your hypothesis about your impact on the work of the group, ask an open ended appreciative question that could provide information to test your hypothesis.	Share in a non-judgmental way the impact of the meeting on your ability to join in the work. Use a positive, appreciative focus.	Make an observation out loud about how a group member's exercise of B/ART is negatively impacting the work of the meeting.

Hold Neutral Facilitator Role

A critical element of the RBF method is that groups own and act on decisions. To ensure that the decision making authority is exercised by the group and not inappropriately held by a facilitator, RBF has a specific skill that defines how the facilitator role is held in meetings.

Awareness	Application	Mastery
Knows the role of neutral facilitator and is aware of what it takes not to seek one's own personal agenda • Do I employ specific practices to maintain the neutral facilitator role and not use the authority of the facilitator to pursue my own agenda?	Holds the neutral role most of the time • Do I refrain from using my expertise or authority to influence group decisions? • Do I recognize when I am not holding the neutral facilitator role?	Consistently holds the neutral role • Do I have a repertoire of practices to acknowledge lapses and return to neutral?

In addition to clarifying the role, authority, and task of the group and the group members, the mental model of B/ART provides a framework to establish the role of a neutral facilitator. The role of the neutral facilitator is central to RBF tools and methods. Holding a neutral role requires the facilitator to give the work back to the group and not use his or her authority to pursue a own personal agenda. The neutral facilitator role makes it possible for the group members to answer their own questions and make their own decisions.

The neutral facilitator role can be held by one person for the duration of the meeting — either a member of the group authorized to hold that role or someone who is an outside facilitator, i.e., someone who is not a member of the group and is invited and

Introduction to RBF

authorized to hold that role. In either instance, holding neutral in an explicit facilitator role occurs when the group authorizes the person to perform specific tasks in support of the group achieving its articulated purpose and within its commonly understood boundaries of time and place.

The agreement regarding the role of the facilitator can be established prior to the meeting, in discussion with the meeting's conveners; at the beginning of the meeting, when the facilitator explicitly asks the group members what they do and don't want from the facilitator; or during the meeting, when either a meeting convener or a participant is authorized by the group to take up the neutral role.

The neutral role requires that the group answer its own questions and prohibits the person holding the neutral role from answering the question for the group. However, that neutrality — i.e., ensuring that whatever answer the group comes up with is their answer — does not extend to a neutrality about meeting results or meeting processes. The neutral role has the task and authority to support the group in achieving meeting results.

In RBF, the concept of B/ART is used to determine whether it is appropriate and/or feasible for a meeting participant or meeting convener to hold the neutral role. Developing the competency to hold the neutral role and knowing when and how to play that role can be both challenging and rewarding.

Groups want neutral facilitators. In hundreds of facilitation workshops, when participants are asked to describe the characteristics of an effective facilitator, they always describe in some way their desire for a facilitator to play a neutral role. When asked what they want from the facilitator their answers group as show in Table 2.

And the people will say, we did it ourselves.
— Lao Tsu

Table 2: What Groups Want and Don't Want From a Facilitator

Groups almost always want	Groups sometimes want	Groups never want
Focus on task within time	Relationship building	A facilitator with his or her own agenda
Movement	Synthesis	
Inclusive participation	Observations	

B/ART for the Neutral Facilitator

The role of neutral facilitator takes place within the specific boundaries of authority, role, and task. The Table 3 describes the B/ART of the neutral facilitator.

Table 3: Facilitator's B/ART

RBF Boundary	time, territory	for the meeting, a segment of a meeting, a series of meetings, formal or informal interactions of people convened or gathered for a purpose
of Authority	the right to do work	from the group to the facilitator (e.g., the group authorizes the role of the facilitator to support them in accomplishing meeting results)
of Role	the function of the person	a neutral role (e.g., giving the work back to the group in a way that the group can do its work within the RBF framework), framing questions, synthesizing the group's answers, offering mental models for the group to use, and not inserting his or her own answers
of Task	the work of the group	relational and analytic, listening and speaking around a series of tasks (e.g., facilitating conversations that add up to the group owning its action in a way that produces results outside the meeting)

> **Reflective Practice: Neutral Facilitator Role**
> - Have you ever been in a meeting that felt as though the facilitator had a personal agenda?
> - What was your reaction?
> - What was the reaction of the group?

The facilitator is working to support the group in doing its work and learning from the experiences that people are having in the meeting. The underlying premise is that groups can learn from their experience and create the capacity within the group to move to effective action. Bion's work on groups highlighted the importance of the facilitator being able to hold steady in his or her role while simultaneously experiencing and reflecting on the experience of what is occurring in group.[8]

A clear understanding of the facilitator's B/ART makes it more likely that the facilitator will hold role and support the group in learning from experience.

Holding Neutral: What Is Your Practice?

Holding a neutral role is not only challenging, but it is also sometimes not appropriate. In most roles it is appropriate to advance a point of view and to exercise your authority to influence or make decisions and get things done. Being aware of how you are not neutral in other roles can support you in being able to hold the neutral role when necessary. This awareness will also help you notice that when you are challenged to hold the neutral role, it may be because consciously or unconsciously you are drawn to another role, e.g., the role of consultant with the authority of expertise or the role of supervisor with the ability to tell people what to do. In the following exercise, examine the examples of how to hold neutral.

Exercise: Holding Neutral
Consider how difficult holding neutral would be for you in a variety of roles, situations, and settings.
Holding neutral entails
Setting aside one's own interests in the outcome of a conversation or meeting
Creating space for people to speak without regard to personal preference or other factors that can skew participation
Giving the work of problem solving and decision making back to the group
Not expressing agreement or disagreement with your favored or disfavored point of view verbally or non-verbally
Being appreciative to points of view that you disagree with
Using a focus on meeting results to enable the group to make choices about the content and sequence of their work
Declaring when you are no longer able to hold neutral

Participant Practice Guide — Hold Neutral Facilitator Role

No Risk	Low Risk	Medium Risk	High Risk
Listen and ask questions from a neutral stance.	Synthesize a conversation out loud in a neutral way.	Chart a few key points of the conversation; capture them in a neutral way.	Volunteer to hold the neutral role for a conversation or a meeting.

---

[8] Young. *Bion and Experiences in Group.* http:/human-nature.com/rmyoung/papers/pap148h.html.

Introduction to RBF

Give the Work Back to the Group

Awareness	Application	Mastery
Understands the role of the facilitator in giving the work back to the group	Applies a repertoire of methods to give the work back to the group	Consistently gives the work back to the group
• Do I refer questions about the work back to the group? • Do I patiently hold the neutral facilitator role while the group takes time to find its own solutions and make its own decisions?	• Do I recognize pivotal moments when to give the work back to the group? • Do I go to the balcony to invite group awareness and insights for forward movement?	• Do I use observation, inquiry, and reflective practice to invite the group to move forward? • Do I use humor, physical activity, intuition, spiritual awareness, and analytical insights to illuminate the group's capacity to do its hardest work?

Giving the work back to the group is an essential skill in maintaining the neutral facilitator role. It is a difficult skill to master since we all want to help solve problems. However, the group must answer its own questions and not look to the facilitator to answer them for the group. The Acknowledge, Rephrase, Explore (ARE) technique is a core method to give the work back to the group.[9]

ARE — A Method to Give Work Back to the Group

Acknowledge: Body language conveys listening.

- ✓ Lean forward
- ✓ Offer a little listening noise.
- ✓ Demonstrate attention through nonverbal cues.

Rephrase: Empathetic responses address feelings.

- ✓ Use your own words to reflect your understanding.
- ✓ Validate that what was heard is what was said.

Explore: Ask open-ended questions to members of the group to gain deeper understanding and to help them address their own issues.

The ability to give work back to the group is often challenging when you have strong opinions or emotions about the topic that the group is addressing. The following exercise is designed to give you practice using ARE, even in the face of strong opinions or emotions. Using ARE in a practice setting helps you use it during meetings to give work back to the group.

---

[9] Courtesy of Steven Jones and Victoria Goddard-Truitt.

Introduction to RBF

Exercise: ARE

With a learning partner, i.e., someone who will work with you to develop skill, use the following five steps to practice ARE. The exercise usually takes about 20 minutes from beginning to end.

1. Review the elements of ARE and the SBI method of feedback.
2. Choose a hot button topic on which the two of you disagree and have strong feelings about. A hot button topic is one that evokes strong emotions in both the speaker and the listener. Hot-button topics often reflect people's values or beliefs about controversial issues. You will each have a chance to facilitate the conversation by using ARE while listening to your learning partner talk about the topic. Decide who will be the facilitator first.
3. The first facilitator uses ARE while his or her learning partner talks about the topic for five minutes.
4. After 5 minutes, the facilitator self-assesses his or her use of ARE and ability to remain neutral and give the work back to the learning partner, and the learning partner offers feedback using the SBI approach.
5. The learning partner now becomes the facilitator and repeats steps 3 and 4 on the same topic.

Participant Practice Guide — Give the Work Back to the Group

No Risk	Low Risk	Medium Risk	High Risk
When you have senior authority or in-depth expertise, listen to others with lesser authority or expertise with curiosity about their point of view.	Ask an open ended question that will generate discussion and engagement of everyone in the group.	Synthesize all the points of view you have heard in the conversation out loud and ask the group what options they might propose to move the group forward.	Go to the balcony and name out loud the roles that people are playing in the conversation and ask people what action is needed to move forward.

Introduction to RBF

HOLD CONVERSATIONS COMPETENCY

Listen with openness, curiosity, and attentiveness to frame dialogues that achieve meeting results.

The use of RBF skills in many roles depends on an ability to listen with openness and appreciation in a specific way that supports the movement from talk to action. Holding conversations is something we all do every day. However, developing the competency to hold conversations that move from talk to action requires conscious and consistent practice. The Holding Conversations competency is developed by practicing two skills:

1. Demonstrate appreciative openness
2. Use Context Statement, Effective Questions, and Listen Fors

Listening looks easy, but it's not simple. Every head is a world.
— Cuban Proverb

The first skill is the ability to demonstrate appreciative openness by listening with curiosity, and attentiveness to thoughts, feelings, and expressions of everyone in a meeting. The second skill is the ability to frame conversations to focus both the listening and the speaking of meeting participants, enabling them to be on the same page at the same time and hear each others' perspectives and points of view.

Demonstrate Appreciative Openness

Awareness	Application	Mastery
Understands the primacy of listening as a skill and is aware of and monitors own listening behavior	Attends to participants to ensure all ideas and voices are heard	Consistently demonstrates interest in conversations of others throughout the meeting
• Am I genuinely curious about the conversation and what is being said? • Am I aware of when I am consciously listening and when I am not? • Do I make conscious choices about when to speak and when to listen?	• Am I aware of filters that may influence what is heard and what is not heard for myself and others? • Do I use strategies to remain open and appreciative and in the moment? • Do I use nonverbal cues of attentiveness and interest? • Do I ask effective questions (EQs) to gain insight into assumptions, facts, and points of view and verify understanding of what was said?	• Do I keep my own interests and interpretations in check (be neutral) when I am listening? • Do I use a variety of strategies to engage speaker (e.g., silence, non-verbal, EQ). • Do I quickly notice lack of listening; acknowledge the lack, and self correct? • Do I maintain focused listening for the duration of a meeting?

The fundamental importance of appreciative listening becomes apparent if you have ever had the misfortune of being in a meeting in which people are not listening to each other and the facilitator is not a good listener. Frustration builds as the conversations become increasingly repetitive, perhaps overly loud, as people try to be heard, or become overly quiet, as people disengage when they realize they are not being heard. The antidote to not being heard is to develop the skill of listening in such a way that people *are* heard, *know* that they are heard, and *are encouraged* to hear others.

Awareness of how you listen and practice appreciative listening is necessary to hold the neutral role. Appreciative listening also enhances your ability to communicate effectively in other roles. Practicing appreciative listening requires commitment and a baseline for improvement. Use the following Appreciative Listening Checklist[10] to establish your baseline for practice.

Appreciative Listening Checklist #1

Consider to what extent you display these characteristics when you are in conversations. Also, consider how your listening might change depending on your role — when you are a participant, a facilitator, or a meeting chair.

Being quiet while the other person is talking,	
Being attentive to the speaker by not performing other tasks,	
Looking at the person who is speaking,	
Being aware of tone, facial expressions, and words, and	
Thinking about what the speaker is saying, rather about what you want to say next.	

Are there other ways that you display appreciative listening? As you consider your own current practice of appreciative listening, consider how persistently and how frequently you are in that state of appreciative listening. Most people without intention and attention are only intermittently fully present in their listening.

Appreciative Listening Checklist #2

Take the opportunity to notice the quality of your listening in meetings by using this checklist. Review the actions listed in the checklist and choose one to try in the moment to increase your skill of appreciative listening.

Do I need to ...	
... stop talking?	
... imagine the other person's viewpoint?	
... look, act, and be interested?	
... observe nonverbal behavior?	
... not interrupt; sit still past my tolerance level?	
... listen between the lines?	
... speak only affirmatively while listening?	
... ensure understanding through rephrasing key points?	
... stop talking; take a vow of silence once in a while?	

Participant Practice Guide — Demonstrate Appreciative Openness

No Risk	Low Risk	Medium Risk	High Risk
Take opportunities in all conversations to listen openly and with curiosity.	Use MBTI awareness regarding your own communication and listening preferences to explore what is easy and hard to hear.	Observe body language and affect of those in meetings; inquire to explore the meaning of what your observe.	Identify absence of hearing each other in a meeting and share a hypothesis re the barrier to listening.

---

[10] http://appreciativeinquiry.case.edu/uploads/whatisai.pdf is a helpful reference for effective questions that facilitate appreciative listening.

Introduction to RBF

Use Context Statement (CS), Effective Questions (EQs), And Listen Fors (LFs)

Being appreciatively open in conversations positions you to be aware of and understand what is said and what is meant in conversations. The skill of using a context statement, asking effective questions[11], and listening with focused intent enables you to take what your are hearing and use that knowledge to frame dialogues. Framing dialogues makes it possible for people to be in the same conversation at the same time and use that common focus to address issues constructively.

Awareness	Application	Mastery
Understands and uses CS, EQs, LFs as a core technique for facilitating	Frames the work (purpose, focus, boundary) with a CS, EQ, and LF in the moment	Regularly uses CS, EQs, and LFs to accelerate a group's ability to achieve meeting results
• Do I set a context to focus a conversation on a meeting result? • Do I prepare EQs in advance to engage people, focus discussion, and move conversations forward towards meeting results? • Do I integrate a CS, with an EQ and link it to an LF?	• Do I use EQs (open ended, inquisitive) to engage people, focus conversations, and to move conversations forward towards meeting results? • Do I listen for responses and incorporate them into the group's work by setting another CS and linked EQ?	• Do I use CS, EQs, LFs to understand the group's experience of pace and adjust the pace to sustain maximum engagement? • Do I use awareness of differential impact (as informed by MBTI and B/ART) in CS, EQs, LFs? • Do I flexibly modify or change a CS, EQs, LFs in the moment based on my reading of the group?

What you say to start a conversation and how you listen to a conversation can be practiced by using this skill. The skill of making a context statement, asking an effective question, and knowing what to listen for enables you and others to all be in the same focused conversation at the same time. A Context Statement (CS), Effective Question (EQ), and Listen For (LF) are used together to frame and facilitate conversations.

> **Reflective Practice: CS, EQs, and LFs**
> Reflect on the following questions:
> - Do I set the context using an easily understood statement?
> - Am I able to use effective questions to clarify and focus the discussion?
> - Am I able to identify Listen Fors?
> - Am I able to consciously hear what I am listening for?

Context Statement
"The purpose of this conversation is to decide the agenda for our next meeting"

Effective Question	Listen For
What do we need to do at our next meeting to move forward?	• topics, • issues, and • decisions to be made

---

[11] Effective Questions were developed as a concept and skill by Oakley and Krug. The definition and many of the examples of effective questions can be found in *Leadership Made Simple*.

Introduction to RBF

You can facilitate any conversation if you make a context statement, ask effective questions, and listen for the key responses.

The Context Statement helps people know what the conversation is about and helps them all be in the same conversation at the same time. Here is an example of a context statement:

> *The purpose of this conversation is to identify what each person can contribute to the strategy.*

The context statement signals to the participants what they want to accomplish in the conversation *and* how they will accomplish it. For example:

> *In this 10 minute conversation, you will have an opportunity to brainstorm ideas about what is contributing to the success of this program.*

The context statement gives a focus and sets a boundary for the conversation.

The Effective Question ignites the conversation and engages people in sharing information and listening to each other. Effective questions are:

- open ended (i.e., not answered merely with yes or no)
- inquisitive (i.e., ask what or how?)
- you-oriented (i.e., What do you think about ...? or How do you feel about ...?), and
- appreciative (i.e., trusting that the person has the answer).

The Listen For is what you consciously have in mind, to hear the essence of how people are responding to the effective question. In practicing the skill, be conscious of and able to name what you are listening for. The Listen For is an intentional filter held flexibly — never to block out what may not fit — rather to focus on the essence of the conversation. A sharply tuned Listen For supports people and the group in hearing the heart of the matter more clearly. The skills of using Context Statement, Effective Questions, and Listen For are an integrated set.

Using the *Context Statement, Effective Questions, Listen Fors* together support the group in having focused conversations that move toward meeting results.

Tips for Using the Skill of CS, EQs, and LFs

- Always state the context at the beginning of the conversation.
- Use the effective question as the header for the flip chart.
- If people are addressing other questions or a different topic, create a separate flip chart as a parking lot for issues or conversations that are not focused on the EQ and/or within the context of the conversation.
- When necessary, use the parking lot to let the group members review and then choose which conversations they want to have when.
- Adjust the context statement and the EQ in the moment to reflect those choices.

Participant Practice Guide — Use Context Statement, Effective Questions, Listen Fors

No Risk	Low Risk	Medium Risk	High Risk
In your own communication, use CS/EQ/LF.	At the beginning of a conversation, flip chart the context and the EQ.	Use what you are listening for to summarize the content and effect of a challenging conversation.	Propose a conversation context and effective question designed to address the underlying cause of a conflict.

HOLD GROUPS COMPETENCY

Support groups in having focused conversations that move to results.

In RBF, the facilitator equipped with the competencies to hold roles and conversations can then deploy a set of skills that enable groups to hold focused conversations. Below are a set of meeting skills that support groups in being in the same conversation at the same time with the capacity to track what is occurring in a conversation and build on ideas, move from idea to idea, or segue from one meeting result to another, and begin and end meetings that move from talk to action.

The following five Hold Groups skills, when used with mastery, support groups in doing common work:

1. Use flip chart to display group's work
2. Sequence
3. Summarize
4. Synthesize
5. Check-in and check-out

Use Flip Chart To Display Group's Work

Awareness	Application	Mastery
Displays group's work accurately	Displays group's work to focus on meeting results	Displays group's work to accelerate progress toward achieving meeting results
• Do people read what is captured? Is it accurate? • Do I use the Context Statement, Effective Questions and Listen Fors to inform what is captured? • Does the speaker recognize what was said in what I captured? • Do I easily capture parallel conversations and accurately record decisions?	• Do my charts serve as a tool to recap work for summary? • Do I use techniques (color, underlining, symbols, spacing, lines) to highlight, track, and distinguish conversations? • Do people who were not in the conversation know its content from what is charted? • Do group members look at and refer to my charts?	• Do my charts support the building of proposals and making decisions? • Does my charting support synthesis and movement toward meeting results? • Do my charts support accountability for action during and after the meeting?

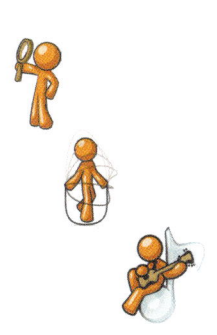

Most people find it easier to follow conversations if there is something visual that provides a focus. Flip charting (or using a white board) provides that focus by recording the key points of what is said, decisions, issues, options, and proposals. Some key benefits of using a flip chart (or white board) are that it:

✓ lets people know they've been heard;
✓ provides a visible running record;
✓ keeps everyone on track;
✓ later provides information to people who were not there (in the form of legible charts and/or typed notes of the charts);
✓ reinforces that there is one conversation;
✓ illuminates the context/effective question/listen for of the conversation;
✓ allows a group to choose among and sequence multiple conversations; and
✓ organizes information to support summary and synthesis.

Flip charting requires knowledge and practice. The tips below outline some of the things you can do to make your flip charts not only legible but also useful to group.

Tips: Using the Flip Chart to Display the Group's Work Accurately

Use the proper tools and technique

The basic tools are colored markers, flip chart pads, easels, and tape.

- Keep all the recorder's tools in a special box or tote bag so you don't forget anything.
- Make sure that whatever is being recorded is clearly visible to the whole group. For example, if possible, use alternating dark colors to separate ideas, and only use red or light colors for emphasis. (Red and light colors are difficult for some people to read across the room.)
- Use wide or wedge-tipped markers for thicker lines.
- Make the letters at least 2–3 inches tall, and leave white space between lines and words.[12]

Work effectively with the group.

- Listen hard at all times.
- Remain neutral. When you pick up the marker, you are picking up the neutral role. This is similar to when a doctor puts on a white coat. Picking up the marker is your reminder to hold neutral. Also, by passing the marker to someone else so he or she can record when you are not neutral, you build the capacity of the group to do its work.
- Ask the group to repeat or clarify as necessary.
- Accept corrections graciously.
- If you are cofacilitating and charting for another facilitator, use the context statement/effective questions/listen fors of the facilitator to organize the information on the chart.
- Always put the context statement or the effective questions at the top of the chart to focus the group's conversation. Use the listen fors to label what is being captured.
- Take the opportunity to gesture toward the flip chart or point out what is recorded to support the group's focus.

Decide what to record.

- Write down what is often called the *group memory*. Depending on the specific meeting result, group memory can include questions, answers, insights, concerns, feedback, ideas from brainstorming sessions. Always record decisions and commitments of who will do what when.
- If in doubt, it's all right to ask something like, "Should I be writing that down?" or "How can I best capture that on paper?" The idea is to work with the group to help you decide what to record.

Record effectively.

- Write large, legibly, and quickly. Put headers on each sheet and number your sheets.
- Don't try to write every word. Use abbreviations recognizable to the group and don't write small words like *the*. Write mainly nouns and verbs.
- Only paraphrase when you are confident the speaker will recognize the paraphrasing. Do not paraphrase as a way to avoid writing controversial statements. Charting helps a group see and address differences and disagreements.
- Don't attribute points to individuals (i.e., do not write down names) unless attribution is important to the work (e.g, who will do what).
- Be sensitive to cultural norms and boundaries of civility. Acknowledge when you are not capturing information in order to respect the norms of civil discourse or the group.
- Don't worry about spelling. You can write the *sp* symbol by any word you are unsure of or invite the group to edit your charts later.
- Use color, symbols, and underlining to highlight points. Make clear when there is a list of topics or ideas that can support a summary.

---

[12] Use references such as book *Flip Charts: How to Draw Them and How Use Them* by Richard C. Brandt to learn more about tools and techniques.

Participant Practice Guide — Flip Charting

No Risk	Low Risk	Medium Risk	High Risk
Practice printing legibly every day as you make notes, journal, or in other ways as you write things down. Make the shape of your letters uniform and clear.	Use a flip chart in one-on-one work conversations and listen for the key points, then practice jotting them down as legibly as possible.	Offer to chart in larger meetings if charting is a norm in the culture.	Offer to chart, if charting is not a norm. (This may require you to bring the flip chart and the markers or use a white board.)

Sequence, Summarize, Synthesize

The three skills of sequencing, summarizing, and synthesizing support groups in holding focused conversations—conversations that have a beginning, a middle, and an end—and that build toward a conversation result. *Conversation results* are the products of a group holding a common task together.

For example, if the task is brainstorming ideas, then the conversation result is a full and expansive list of ideas that reflect the contributions of all members, not limited by any member's preconceived ideas or critical judgement. The skills of sequencing, summarizing, and synthesizing contribute to groups holding conversations that lead to action.

Sequence

Awareness	Application	Mastery
Understands and practices sequencing speakers	Understands and practices sequencing topics or ideas	Understands and practices sequencing the work of meetings and meeting results
• Do I establish who speaks when in a way that is clear to the group and enables participants to relax and listen?	• Do I recognize different topics or conversations, label them, and invite the group to choose which conversation to have when?	• Do I recognize opportunities for proposals, decisions, and commitments to action and invite the group to sequence them during the meeting to accomplish meeting results?

Groups often circle, spin, and frustrate themselves because people cannot get their voices into the conversation, because multiple conversations are occurring at the same time, or because the group members can't organize their conversations so they can take steps in the work that build toward a conversation or meeting result. Establishing a sequence of speakers, conversations, and work helps groups move forward together.

Sequencing Speakers

People can only attend to one voice at a time. Sequence the speakers to support the group holding one conversation at a time.

Ask that those who want to speak raise their hands. Make a list of speakers and call them in order—or more informally, give them numbers and have them remember their number in the sequence. After establishing a sequence, ask if anyone else wants to speak. Watch for nonverbal cues and respond with a nonverbal acknowledgment (e.g., a nod) to let people know they are in the sequence. Build the group's confidence by assuring them that they will be able to pay attention to the conversation and not have to worry about whether they will get an opportunity to speak.

Sometimes certain members do not respect the sequencing — perhaps breaking in on other speakers and/or speaking out of turn. How the facilitator responds to out-of-sequence participation varies based on the context and the group culture. However, here are some factors that can inform the facilitator's response:

- ✓ Often group members with high levels of hierarchical authority test the facilitator's authority. The facilitator's role is to treat all group members as equals, and therefore, the preferred response is to work to hold the sequence and acknowledge when that is not accepted by those with higher authority.

- ✓ Extroverted, highly engaged, or argumentative members may ignore sequence as they respond to every comment or idea offered. The facilitator works to hold back their comments (*Do you mind waiting until X or Y has spoken?*) and tests whether the group wants to pause the sequence to have a deeper conversation on the issue under discussion.

- ✓ Aggrieved or hostile members may ignore sequence. The facilitator can attend to the underlying intent of the comments and use inquiry to identify the source of the conflict and support the group's capacity to directly address the conflict.

Participant Practice Guide — Sequencing

No Risk	Low Risk	Medium Risk	High Risk
Notice when there is a lack of sequencing of speakers in a meeting. Raise your hand and indicate your willingness to wait your turn.	Observe verbal and non-verbal cues of members wanting to speak. Make a mental list. When you speak, acknowledge the others who are waiting. When you have finished speaking turn to the person next in the sequence.	Make notes of the issues, topics, or conversations that are occurring simultaneously. When you speak, label your own topic, issue, or conversation and connect it or distinguish it from the other conversations, issues, or topics.	When a group is frustrated with their lack of progress, consider what is missing that prevents forward motion. Name what is missing and propose that the group deal with that issue first so it can move forward.

Summarize

Awareness	Application	Mastery
Remembers and can list ideas from short conversations	Remembers and can list categories of topics from medium to long conversations	Remembers and can briefly list process description or meeting results from a whole meeting
• Do I have a way to practice hearing, accurately remembering, and restating as a list ideas that emerge from a conversation?	• Do I concisely and accurately describe the content of conversations? • Do my summaries move a group forward towards the meeting results?	• Do I mentally review and then concisely state what has occurred in the meeting and the results achieved?

For groups to move from talk to action, they need to know where they are in a conversation and, from that knowledge, figure out how to move to the next step of work. When engaged fully in a conversation, group members may forget or lose track of the thread of meaning in the conversation, so they would find it helpful to have a list of ideas shared, options identified, or decisions made.

Reflective Practice: Summarizing

Summarizing a list of ideas is possible when you are conscious of what you are listening for and staying focused on ideas while listening for the length of a whole conversation.

- How well do you summarize ideas now?
- Can you readily list ideas you have heard?
- What is a practice you might adopt to strengthen your ability to summarize ideas?

Participant Practice Guide — Summarizing

No Risk	Low Risk	Medium Risk	High Risk
Make notes to yourself of what you hear in conversations. Look at your notes and name the lists that form the content summary of the conversations.	In a meeting, use your notes to offer a summary of the conversation thus far as a context for what you want to add to the conversation.	Offer to share your notes electronically after the meeting so the group has a summary of the ideas, decisions, or commitments going forward.	At the end of a meeting, offer a summary of what has been accomplished in the meeting and what people have committed to.

Synthesize

Awareness	Application	Mastery
Briefly states the meaning of short conversations - Do I listen for the central meaning of the conversation and state that concisely? - Do I use basic methods of synthesis (comparison, themes, part/whole connections) in listening for and concisely stating where the group is in their work?	Integrates and briefly states the meaning of a number of conversations or longer conversations - Does the group affirm my synthesis and use it to move forward to meeting results? - Do I use images and symbolism to help the group own the results of a whole meeting?	Integrates and briefly states the meaning for a whole meeting - Does my synthesis accelerate the group's work? - Does the group use my synthesis to move to action?

This is the skill that brings the parts of a conversation or meeting together and offers a thread of common meaning that represents the whole. *Synthesis* combines the parts into a unified whole; synthesis gets at the heart of the matter. Synthesizing is a more advanced skill than summarizing. Summarizing compiles or lists what occurred. Summarizing requires attention, memory, and focus to ensure that the list is complete.

To synthesize, however, requires a way to name, organize, or identify conversations or meeting results so that people can see the parts as a whole and can use that insight to move forward. Synthesizing supports the group in owning the meaning that has been created in the conversation. It is a step beyond summarizing, though the ability to summarize informs the synthesis.

Participant Practice Guide — Synthesizing

No Risk	Low Risk	Medium Risk	High Risk
Before speaking, consider the essence of what you want to communicate and practice expressing the heart of the matter briefly (in less than a minute).	In a meeting, listen for the parts and hypothesize about what the parts add up to. Share your hypothesis with the group.	Offer to chart a conversation in a way that captures the parts as a whole. Check with the group to see if it is helpful in moving the group forward.	Offer a synthesis of a difficult or confusing conversation that sharpens the group's awareness of an unaddressed issue (elephant in the room) or an implicit assumption.

Check-In And Check-Out

Conversations and meetings have beginnings, middles, and ends. For conversations and meetings to have results that move groups from talk to action, people need to be joined to the work and to each other. They need to acknowledge the endings of conversations and meetings to be able to transition to the next step of taking the action between meetings.

check-in: a process to facilitate connections to the task and with each other so people are ready to work together.

The skill of *checking in* (joining to the work) and *checking out* (transitioning to the next step) is used at the beginning and ending of meetings, respectively, and also during meetings to ensure that people are moving together from conversation to conversation or from one type of work to another.

The *check-in* can be as short as each person saying a brief sentence or a phrase or a word. A *check-out* similarly can be brief. Conversely check-ins and check-outs may be longer and more in-depth. The content and the length of the check-in and check-out are varied, depending on what is needed for the group to do and advance its work.

check-out: process to facilitate the closing of a meeting so people are committed to the group, ready to transition to follow up, and aware of the progress made toward their own results and the meeting results.

Check-in and check-out are sometimes the norm in groups and organizations, and sometimes they are not. As you develop mastery in this skill, you will experiment and find ways to use this skill in ways that are responsive to the needs and expectations of the group.

Awareness	Application	Mastery
Understands and uses check-in and check-out	Connects group members to each other and the meeting results through check-in and check-out	Reads group to inform check-in and check-out
• Does my check-in establish a foundation for the group to own the achievement of meeting results? • Do my check-outs assess meeting results and move people to action?	• Do I consider the relationships of the people to each other and the work in framing the check-in and check-out? • Do my check-ins and check-outs illuminate B/ART and make it more likely that members will contribute their resources to the meeting result? • Do my check-outs address whether meeting results were achieved and elicit how group members felt about the meeting experience?	• Do I use the technique of checking in and out flexibly during a series of conversations, or do I facilitate transitions from one meeting result to another? • Do I use check-in or check-out to explore hypotheses about group dynamics or make the group aware of group dynamics? • Do my check-ins and check-outs at the beginning and end of meetings and the beginning and end of conversations move a group to action?

Check-Ins

Check-ins are ignited with a brief context statement (CS) that names the purpose of the check-in and launches with an effective question (EQ). Connecting people to each other and the work is more effective when check-ins touch on the relational and task dimensions that need to be addressed during the meeting. A check-in can consist of more than one effective question to bring these multiple dimensions into the

Introduction to RBF

awareness of the group and strengthen the groups ability to work together. Up to three or four questions can be posed to the group to frame the check-in. After providing a moment for reflection, each participant includes in his or her check-in statement responses to all three or four questions. It is good practice to provide a brief summary or synthesis of a more complex check-in as a segue to the work of the meeting.

A standard check-in that integrates relational and task dimensions is one that uses three effective questions connect people to each other and to the work. This check-in uses three effective questions in a sequence that starts with how people are feeling and moves to task. Known as *PIT Check-in* it provides a rapid method to begin a meeting with people ready to work together.[13]

Personal: How are you?
Interpersonal: Is there anything between us?
Task: What's the work?

Check-Outs

Check-outs are also ignited with a brief CS that names the purpose of the check-out and poses an EQ that acknowledges the work of the group and transitions the group to next steps and action.

A standard check-out that you can use in many types of meetings allows people to quickly transition from the work of the meeting to the action after the meeting. It is a series of three effective *PIT Questions:*

Personal: How are you right now?
Interpersonal: What do you appreciate about the work of the group?
Task: What is your next step or commitment to action?

Participant Practice Guide — Check-in and Check-out

No Risk	Low Risk	Medium Risk	High Risk
A personal check-in is done informally and lightly, e.g., How are you?	Check-in: Invite people to say what they would like to accomplish in the meeting if task focus is the norm.	Check-out: Invite and/or model and ask others to share something they appreciated about the meeting.	Check-out: Model making commitments to action and next steps and ask others to share their commitments.

---

[13] Bob Hoffman contributed the PIT check-in during the development of the *Resident Leadership and Facilitation Workbook*, www.aecf.org.

Introduction to RBF

Hold 3R Meetings

Use the 3R framework to design and facilitate meetings that move groups from talk to action.

The 3Rs: Relationships, Resources, And Results

Mental models articulate the how and why of the way people do work or the way people could work. They are descriptive and prescriptive. RBF's underlying mental model for designing and executing meetings posits that people who are in relationship with each other and are focused on a common result can work to use their resources (talent, expertise, influence, authority, money, access, goods, services, property) to take action together. The 3R framework is a mental model that is applied in the design and execution of meetings to produce results in programs, organizations, neighborhoods, and communities.

Attending to the relationships and resources of the people and the results they can produce—is the 3R mental model of RBF meeting design and execution. 3R meetings are designed and implemented so that people's relationships plus the resources they bring to the work will add up to results.

Relationships + Resources = Results

The hold 3R meetings competency incorporates two skills -- the skill of designing 3R meetings and the skill of using the 3R framework in meetings to catalyze conversations that move people from talk to effective action.

1. Use the 3Rs (results, relationships, resources) to design the meeting.
2. Use the 3Rs in the meeting to get results.

Applying the 3R Framework

Use the 3R framework to inform the conduct of conversations and the design meetings. For example, in meetings the 3Rs are used to formulate context statements, effective questions, and listen fors to frame conversations. The framework is also used to design meetings. In meeting design, the framework represents a thinking process that can be used by a participant, convener, or facilitator to prepare for a meeting, and/or as an interactive co-design process in which the convener, facilitator, and some or all of the participants work together to develop:

- ✓ the common result that can bring people together;
- ✓ an understanding of how the participants relate to each other and how they relate to the common result; and
- ✓ the resources that the participants have or have access to that could contribute to the result.

In the meeting design process or conversation, exploration can start with any of the 3Rs (relationships, resources, or results); however, it is important to touch on all three. The 3R meeting design is an iterative process in which insights emerge along the way that shape the desired meeting results, the choice of appropriate participants, and the preparation needed for accomplishing the meeting results.

Using the 3R mental model in the two ways described in the paragraph above creates a parallel structure from the level of conversations to the level of whole meetings. This parallel structure allows 3R meetings to be both intentional—prepared for in advance—and responsive and adaptive in the meeting itself. The intentional preparation produces an agenda for the meeting with defined meeting results and a schedule for discussing topics. The responsive and adaptive dimension comes into play during the meeting. For example, if the group needs more or less time to discuss a topic or discovers new issues to discuss, the agenda is adapted to be responsive to the work the group is doing and needs to do to accomplish the meeting results. The use of the 3R framework during the meeting supports the responsive adaptation of the agenda by enabling the group to attend to relationship and resources as they make decisions about what they want to do, how they want to do it and how what they are doing will support them in accomplishing the desired meeting results.

Use the 3Rs to Design the Meeting

Awareness	Application	Mastery
Understands the inter-relationship and use of the 3Rs as they relate to the design of a meeting agenda	Uses EQs and LFs to elicit what the group wants to accomplish, who is and needs to be involved, and what people have and can bring to achieve the desired results	Designs the meeting agenda and environment for the group to own their work by applying the 3Rs
• Do I clearly articulate the results for meetings (specific, observable, measurable)? • Do the proposed meeting results contribute to a program or organizational result?	• Do I use B/ART in analyzing the composition of groups to explore who might be invited to contribute to meeting results? • Do I assess if those invited can accomplish the meeting results with their relationships and resources?	• Do I align meeting preparation and design with the desired results? • Do I ensure that the required resources are accessible at the meeting? • Do I recognize and encourage people aligning their resources to achieve results?

What are Meeting Results?

In developing the 3R competency, the first step is to have a clear understanding of what meetings results are and to have a method for developing and articulating them. Meeting results are:

- ✓ produced when the work of the participants in a meeting is successful,
- ✓ the product of constructive, focused conversations (i.e., conversation results produce meeting results),
- ✓ specific, observable, and measurable; you can tell whether the results occurred or not,
- ✓ varied by the type of work being done and the capacity of the group to address issues and move to action,

- ✓ cumulative and build toward accomplishing the meeting purpose, and
- ✓ connected to a meeting purpose that is a step along the way to the program, organizational, or community results.

What are the most common types of meeting results?

The ability to articulate meeting results that are specific, measurable, and observable and that contribute to a program or organizational result (e.g., the necessary work occurs outside of or between meetings), is helpful in moving to action. Examples of the most common meeting results can aid you in developing this skill.

The Meeting Result Guide in Table 4 defines twelve meeting results typical of the work groups do to move from talk to action. For each of the twelve types of meeting results, there are three examples of how to articulate that result along a continuum of low to high impact. A high impact meeting result is one that is almost certain to help the group move to action. In developing this skill, strive to articulate meeting results in as high impact a way as possible. Keep in mind that the low and medium impact results can be valuable when used as building blocks to the achievement of high impact meeting results.

Select the Meeting Results

After defining purpose, review the meeting results guide to select the meeting results that will move the group toward achieving the meeting purpose. Use the Meeting Result Guide to help you articulate the results selected in a way that is more likely to move the group to action. If the results you are looking for are not listed in the Guide, use the examples in the Guide to inform how you articulate the additional meeting results.

When you select meeting results, always include the first meeting result (Ready to work together) to begin meetings, and the last result (Commitments to action made) for the end of meetings. Including these two results ensures that you will come with meeting results in mind and leave with action commitments in hand. Often the check-in is designed to achieve the Ready to work together meeting result and the check-out is designed to achieve the Commitments to action made meeting result.

Formulate the Meeting Results

Formulate meeting results that are:

- ✓ Clear and specific: *Can I describe the desired result so others will understand?*
- ✓ Observable: *Will I be able to tell if the result happened or not?*
- ✓ Meaningful: *Will accomplishing this result make important and valuable progress toward our ultimate goals for the work?*
- ✓ Feasible: *Do I honestly believe we can achieve this result? Do we have sufficient influence and/or resources to achieve this result?*

The Meeting Results Guide provides examples of meeting results along a continuum from low impact to high impact. The examples may stretch you to formulate more impactful meeting results or to see how achieving a lower-impact meeting result can be a step along the way to achieving a higher-impact meeting result. Once your meeting results are clear, you can sequence them and include them in an agenda.

Table 4: Meeting Results Guide

Type of Meeting Result	Low Impact	Medium Impact	High Impact
Ready to work together Establish a foundation of an agreed upon set of results that are important to the participants and confirm that the participants are committed to each other and their task.	Know each other's names and roles.	Reach mutual agreement on results and identify each person's interest in the group and its work.	Understand how the roles, authority, and resources each person brings will contribute to achieving mutually agreed-on results.
Relationships strengthened Foster active participation, open communication, and effective collaboration.	Agree on norms related to working well together.	Hold each other accountable for adhering to norms.	Candidly explore differing perspectives and confidently address difficult/sensitive issues.
Information shared Transfer knowledge to advance the work.	Provide status reports or educational presentations.	Discuss potential relevance of knowledge transfer for the work.	Identify implications from knowledge transfer and use to advance the work.
Ideas generated Brainstorm and explore possibilities.	List new ideas.	Identify which new ideas to explore.	Prioritize new ideas using agreed-on criteria.
Problem solved Overcome obstacles to advance the work.	Identify causes and brainstorm ideas to address them.	Evaluate ideas and develop robust recommendations for solving problem.	Make commitments to implement selected solutions.
Feedback/input secured Gather information to improve the work.	Share feedback and/or improvement suggestions.	Explore feedback and identify implications for work.	Agree on revisions to work in response to feedback.
Strategy/Action Plan developed Decide what to do to achieve results.	Identify potential activities.	Define desired destination and key steps to get there.	Sequence and schedule actions, identifying any critical path dependencies.
Decisions made Make choices together about what to do.	Make a decision.	Each person commits to support the decision.	Hold each other accountable for implementing the decision.
Conflict resolved Address dynamics that inhibit progress.	Acknowledge and describe conflict.	Identify and explore sources of conflict.	Commit to actions to resolve conflict.
Accountability strengthened Publicly report progress on commitments.	Report progress on commitments.	Report progress and identify areas needing improvement.	Report progress and problem solve how to either get back on track or sustain momentum.
Progress recognized Acknowledge what has been accomplished.	Review milestones.	Celebrate progress or admit lack of progress on milestones.	Include key stakeholders in celebration or postmortem.
Commitments to action made Publicly say who will do what by when.	Say who will do what.	Say who will do what by when.	Say who will do what by when and set quality expectations.

Participant Practice Guide — Use the 3Rs to design the meeting

No Risk	Low Risk	Medium Risk	High Risk
Be prepared to introduce a conversation that illuminates the resources the group has to achieve the meeting results.	Contact the meeting convener prior to the meeting and use EQs to clarify your understanding of the meeting results.	At the beginning of the meeting, share a proposal about how to sequence meeting topics accomplish the meeting results.	Offer to take the lead in developing a 3R agenda for a group.

Use the 3Rs in the Meeting to Achieve Results

Awareness	Application	Mastery
Understands the inter-relationships and use of the 3Rs to help groups achieve results • Do the meeting results align with the meeting purpose? • Do all the meeting results add up to the purpose?	Uses EQs and LFs with group to elicit their 3Rs during the meeting • Do the CS, EQs. and LFs achieve the meeting result?	Creates an environment for the group to own their work by applying the 3Rs; captures decisions, commitments, etc., in a 3R framework • Do I use the 3R framework to follow up on meetings to move from talk to action? • Do I capture decisions and commitments in terms of who will do what when, how, and with whom, and with what resources?

PRODUCTIVE MEETINGS

Productive meetings align the meeting purpose and results, the meeting participants, and the meeting design. Thinking about the meeting participants from a person-role-system perspective and in relationship to the meeting results is a way of understanding group dynamics and is called a composition analysis.

The following questions can clarify tasks that enable people to prepare for and conduct productive meetings.

- Who will attend the meeting and how can they contribute to the meeting results?
- What information do they have and what information do they need to participate effectively?
- What is the meeting design that will engage the participants in the work of the meeting?

Use the following All-in-One Agenda template to prepare for meetings, guide the work of meetings and document the progress made in meetings.

Participant Guide — Use the 3Rs in the Meeting to Achieve Results

No Risk	Low Risk	Medium Risk	High Risk
Prior to the start of a meeting, make note of one result that you want from the meeting. If the opportunity arises, engage fully in discussions related to that result.	At the beginning of a meeting, name what result you would like from the meeting and ask others to name theirs.	During a meeting leverage your relationships to encourage others to contribute the resources they control or influence to achieve a result.	Use inquiry to illuminate any relationship issues that are barriers to moving to action.

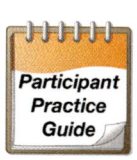

Introduction to RBF

Using the 3Rs for Your Meeting

Think about an upcoming meeting that you will be responsible for planning and/or facilitating and fill-in the worksheet below. The meeting could be work related or not.

All-in-One Agenda

Come with meeting results in mind and leave with action commitments in hand

Meeting Title: _____

Date &Time: _____

Location: _____

Meeting Purpose

_____

Meeting results	Accomplished	Some progress	Not addressed	Next steps
Ready to work together				
Action commitments made				

Agenda

Time	Task/Result	Notes: Insights, Decisions, Next Steps
	Task: *Welcome, purpose, check-in* Result: *Ready to work together*	
	Task: Result:	
	Task: Result:	
	Task: *Check-out* Result: *Action commitments made*	
	Adjourn	

Leave with Action Commitments

Who needs to take action?	What actions will move the group forward?	When will the process start and end?	Why is this action a priority?

Agenda, Page 2

Meeting Title: _____

Date &Time: _____

Location: _____

Notes

Composition Analysis

Name	Organization	Role	Contribution/Connection

WHAT NEXT? TRY PBDM.

Using the foundation competencies and their associated skills will help you have meetings that are productive and move from talk to action. These skills may be deployed by you in many roles from facilitator to participant.

There is set of advanced competencies that can not only help move from talk to action in difficult meetings but also help you get population level results. One of the skills in the advanced competency of Hold Mental Models is that of Proposal-based Decision Making (PBDM).

The precursor to doing is deciding; however, groups often get stuck in talk and can't move to action because they cannot make decisions together. Therefore, an explicit mental model for collaborative decision-making is the first skill in the hold mental models competency.

- ✓ A PBDM decision is one everyone supports and no one opposes.
- ✓ A PBDM decision is reached when everyone in the group can say: *I can live with the decision and support it, even though it may not be exactly what I want.*

Many groups have had experience at different times with unstructured consensus decision-making processes and/or with Robert's Rules of Order. Robert's Rules has many strengths in providing a process for group decision making. However, often those in the minority do not own the decision, and therefore, may not support it, and thus emphasis on debate and the criticism of competing ideas may not lead to creative problem solving or the development of ideas that everyone can support.

In contrast to the Robert's Rules advocacy approach to achieve majority support, PBDM uses the mental model of inquiry. Through inquiry, PBDM supports convergence in groups and catalyzes joint problem solving to achieve ownership of the decision by of the entire group. In the PBDM process, people make proposals and build on each other's proposals. Instead of voting yea or nay for a motion, people show their *level* support as follows.

- ✓ Thumbs-up for support,
- ✓ Thumbs sideways for not sure, and
- ✓ Thumbs down for don't support.

People with their thumbs sideways or down are engaged through inquiry to share their issues. They are encouraged to articulate what they need to support a proposal. Everyone in the group then works to address these issues and modifies the initial proposal or develops a new proposal that everyone can support.

Using thumbs to show their level of support for a proposal makes it easier for people to act into the new way of thinking that is the underlying mental model of PBDM. The act of showing where you are and noticing where others are provides information to the individuals in the group that is immediately useful in moving toward convergence. The use of thumbs and the work toward convergence is distinctly different in form and content from other methods of decision making. By using their thumbs people are experiencing a new approach and learning from the experience.

Table 5: The Six-Step PBDM Method

Step	Possible Script Wording
1 Make a proposal.	I propose that …
2 Add to or make a new proposal.	Do you want to add to it or make a new proposal?
3 Show thumbs.	Do you support it? Do you not support it? Are you not sure?
4 Build support.	What will bring your thumb up?
5 All thumbs up !	Proposal adopted!
6 Commit to action.	Who will do what when?

1. Make a proposal.

Take an idea of what you want and use proposal language to make a proposal. Use a calm, constructive tone of voice. *I propose that…* [insert a short phrase describing what you want].

2. Add to or make a new proposal.

Explore whether people want to add to your proposal or make new proposals. Consider the proposals as different options or possible decisions the group might make.

3. See where people are – use a show of thumbs.

Ask people to show where they are by a show of thumbs. Do they support a proposal (thumb up), are they not sure (thumb sideways), or do they not support (thumb down)?

4. Build proposals everyone can support.

Ask people whose thumbs are sideways or down (not sure or don't agree), *What will bring your thumb up?* Listen to their issues and encourage proposals that address the issues. Invite everyone to make proposals that everyone can support. Ask people to do the work of finding convergence.

5. All thumbs up! Decision made!

A proposal is adopted and becomes a decision when everyones, or almost everyone's thumb is up and the group decides they have enough support to move forward because the people whose thumb is not up are okay with the group going forward.

6. Commit to Action.

The group moves to action by deciding who will do what when to implement the decision.

The Language of PBDM

In PBDM, people are either making proposals, building on proposals or making another proposal. The following language of PBDM might includes phrases like:

- ✓ Make a proposal: *I propose that_____.*
- ✓ Build on a proposal: *I would like to build on that proposal by_____.*
- ✓ Make another proposal: *I would like to make another proposal.*

Where to get more information and support for RBF Skills Development?

You can find *Results Based Facilitation: Book One — Foundation Skills* and *Results Based Facilitation: Book Two — Advanced Skills* on *www.rbl-apps.com*. In addition, support for the practice and development of the foundation and advanced skills can be found through the Results Based Facilitation Network. The mission of the network is to support the application and integration of results based facilitation skills. You can connect to this network at *www.rbfnetwork.com*.

APPENDIX A

MEETING DESIGN WORKSHEET

Meeting Design

Think about an upcoming meeting that you will be responsible for planning or facilitating, or in which you will be participating and answer the questions below.

1. **What is the meeting?**

2. **What is the purpose of the meeting?**

3. **What are the desired results of the meeting (what will participants know more about, do, feel, etc., as a result of this meeting)?**

4. **What is the amount of time available?**

5. **Who is coming to the meeting and what are the relationships between the person and other participants and the meeting purpose? (use the back of the page if necessary)**

APPENDIX B
REFLECTIVE PRACTICE JOURNAL

APPENDIX C

INDIVIDUAL DEVELOPMENT PLAN

RBF Competencies and Skills	Skill Level/Continuum		
	Awareness	Application	Mastery
Hold Roles: *be aware of and make choices about roles that contribute to meeting results*			
Use B/ART to define and differentiate roles in relation to meeting results			
Use B/ART to understand group dynamics and achieve meeting results			
Hold neutral facilitator role			
Give the work back to the group			
Next Steps and Commitments:			
Hold Conversations: *listen with curiosity and attentiveness to frame dialogues that move to achieving results*			
Demonstrate appreciative openness			
Use Context Statements, Effective Questions, Listen Fors			
Next Steps and Commitments:			
Hold Groups: *support groups in having focused conversations that move to achieving results*			
Use flip chart to display group's work			
Sequence			
Summarize			
Synthesize			
Check-in and Check-out			
Next Steps and Commitments:			
Hold 3R Meetings: *use the 3Rs to design and facilitate meetings that move groups from talk to action*			
Use the 3Rs to design the meeting			
Use the 3Rs in the meeting to achieve results			
Next Steps and Commitments:			

About the Author

Jolie Bain Pillsbury, Ph.D., President of Sherbrooke Consulting, Inc., is the author of the two book set on Results Based Facilitation. Ms. Pillsbury is a co-founder of the Results Based Facilitation Network and the Results Based Leadership Consortium, a founding co-director of the Results Based Leadership Collaborative at the University of Maryland School of Public Policy.

As a developer and practitioner of Results Based Leadership, she has authored the *Theory of Aligned Contributions*, which serves as the foundation for research and basis for continuous improvement in the effectiveness of results based leadership practice.

For more information visit, www.sherbrookeconsulting.com, www.rbl-apps.com, www.rbfnetwork.com, and www.rblconsortium.com.